The Romans

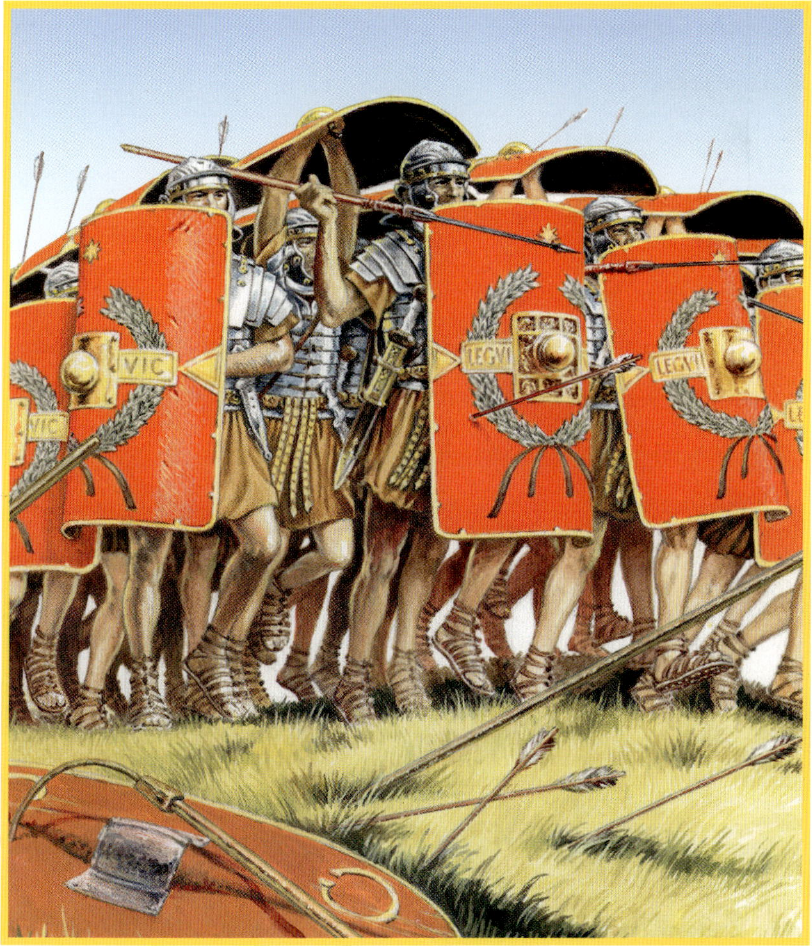

MACMILLAN

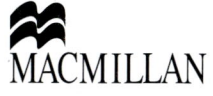

Philip Steele

Macmillan Education
Between Towns Road, Oxford OX4 3PP
A division of Macmillan Publishers Limited
Companies and representatives throughout the world

ISBN 978-0-230-43218-5
ISBN 978-0-230-43062-4 [Spanish edition]

Text, design and illustration © Macmillan Publishers Limited 2012

Text written by Philip Steele

First published 2012

All rights reserved; no part of this publication may be reproduced, stored in a retrieval system, transmitted in any form, or by any means, electronic, mechanical, photocopying, recording, or otherwise, without the prior written permission of the publishers.

Designed by Helen James

Cover and title page photography reproduced with the kind permission of Kingfisher.

The author and publishers would like to thank the following for permission to reproduce their photographic material:
Top = t; Bottom = b; Centre = c; Left = l; Right = r

Art Archive/Archaeological Museum Alexandria/Dagli Orti p13(t), Art Archive/Musee Archaeologique Naples/Alfredo Dagli Orti p27, Art Archive/Musee de la Civilisation Gallo-Romaine Lyon/Gianni Dagli Orti p21(t), **Corbis**/Massimo Borchi p15, Corbis/Roger Ressmeyer p7(b), **Getty**/Joseph Barrak/AFP p28, Getty/Pierre Andrieu/AFP p5; **Shutterstock**/G2019 pp3, 4, Shutterstock/riekephotos pp3, 11, Shutterstock/Rui Vale de Sousa p25, Shutterstock/Sergielev p10(b); All other images from the Kingfisher artbank.

These materials may contain links for third party websites. We have no control over, and are not responsible for, the contents of such third party websites. Please use care when accessing them.

Although we have tried to trace and contact copyright holders before publication, in some cases this has not been possible. If contacted, we will be pleased to rectify any errors or omissions at the earliest opportunity.

Printed and bound in China

2015 2014 2013 2012
10 9 8 7 6 5 4 3 2 1

Llyfrgelloedd Mon, Conwy & Gwynedd Libraries	
Askews & Holts	
AP	8 APR 2014

Contents

Roman treasure	4
Finding out	6
Rome and its empire	8
Buying and selling	10
Soldiers and war	12
Gods and temples	14
At home	16
Food and feasts	18
Getting dressed	20
Entertainment	22
Going to the baths	24
Roman children	26
What happened to Rome?	28
Glossary	30
Index	32

Roman treasure

The Romans ruled most of Europe more than 1,600 years ago. They also ruled many other lands. They came from a big city called Rome, in Italy.

Today we can still find things which the Romans made or used. People find the remains of Roman walls and buildings. They sometimes find old coins, pottery jars or rings and **brooches**. These help us understand how the Romans lived.

Pont du Gard in France

A man brushes away earth in a city called Bordeaux, in France. Underneath he finds a beautiful floor. It dates back to Roman times.

Finding out

In Italy there is a volcano called Mount Vesuvius. It **erupted** in 79AD. There was a big explosion, which buried the town of Pompeii under earth and rock. Many people died.

Vesuvius erupting

Hundreds of years later, people cleared away the earth and rock. They found the Roman houses and streets. There were shops, gardens, markets and theatres. People found pots and pans, and even food. There were fine statues, musical instruments, jewellery and coins. Everyone

The barking dog

At the entrance to one house there was a picture of an angry dog. Under the picture it said 'Beware of the dog'.

could see how the Romans lived. Here are the ruins of Pompeii today.

Rome and its empire

More than 2,700 years ago Rome was just a few villages, built on hills near the River Tiber. The villages joined up to make a town, then the town became a city. This city grew until Rome was the biggest city in the world. About a million people lived there.

The Romans sent armies to **conquer** other lands. They ruled Spain, France, Britain and parts of Germany.

The Romans ruled Romania, Greece, western Asia and North Africa, too. These countries made up the Roman **empire**.

The wolf and the twins
An old **myth** said that a wolf found twin baby boys called Romulus and Remus by the River Tiber. The wolf looked after them. When Romulus grew up, he became the first king of Rome.

The Romans built roads all over the empire.

Buying and selling

The Romans were good businessmen. They used coins made of gold, silver, bronze and copper. At Roman **ports**, they loaded ships with pottery and cloth. There was food and there were jars of wine or olive oil. Traders argued over prices.

This Roman jar held wine or oil.

Roman coins

The Romans bought and sold people too. They owned **slaves**. These people had no freedom and they had to work hard for no money.

Pirate attack!
In 68BC pirates attacked the Roman port of Ostia. The Romans built 500 ships to fight them. They caught many pirates.

Every Roman city had a place called the **forum**. People met here to do business. Around it there were markets and shops.

Soldiers and war

The Roman army had different groups called **legions**. Each legion had its own number and badge. Most soldiers fought on foot, but some fought on horses.

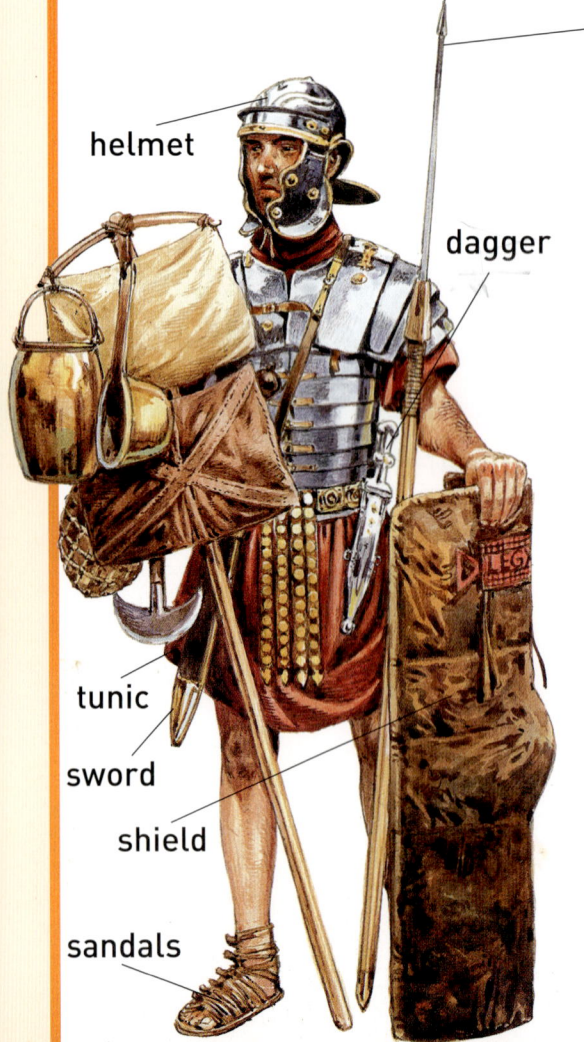

Roman soldiers wore tunics and sandals or boots. They wore helmets and armour, and carried shields. Their weapons were short swords, daggers and spears.

One of the best Roman **generals** was called Julius Caesar. He won many battles for Rome. He became very powerful and people were jealous of him. Some men murdered him in Rome in 44BC.

Julius Caesar

The tortoise
Groups of Roman soldiers sometimes marched close together. They covered their heads and bodies with shields. They looked a bit like a tortoise, protected by a shell.

Gods and temples

The Romans believed in many different gods. Jupiter was the most important god. He was god of the sky. People believed he punished them with a **thunderbolt** when they were bad. Other gods looked after different areas of life, such as war, love or the sea.

A temple in France

The Romans built temples for their gods and had festivals. The festival of Saturn was in the winter. People lit candles, had big feasts and gave presents.

A monster dog
Roman myths are full of monsters. Cerberus was a dog with three heads. He stopped dead people entering the world of the living.

At home

Romans believed that gods and **spirits** protected their homes. They made **offerings** to them every day.

There were many sorts of house. In the biggest cities, such as Rome or Ostia, there were blocks of flats. Many towns had family houses with an open courtyard and pools of water. There were tiles on the roofs and the small windows had shutters.

In the country, rich people owned big houses called **villas**. Some had fine wall paintings or **mosaics** on the floors.

This grand Roman house had lots of rooms, a garden and a courtyard.

Food and feasts

In the kitchen, slaves carried water and wood for the fire. Pots and pans boiled on the stove. Cooks used olive oil, herbs and spices. A main dish might be fish or chicken. There were onions, peas and cabbages, as well as figs and grapes. The Romans sweetened their food and drink with honey.

People did not eat much for breakfast or lunch. The main meal of the day was dinner. Some rich people held **banquets** where everyone ate too much. Guests lay on couches and ate from a low table, using their fingers and knives.

Are you hungry? Guests at a banquet might eat mice cooked in honey or snails in wine.

Getting dressed

A Roman lady spent a long time getting dressed in the morning. She put on a long tunic and then a woollen dress called a **stola** on top. She used perfume and jars of make-up and curled her hair. She wore earrings and necklaces, then looked at herself in a mirror.

Pretty poison
Roman ladies liked to look pale. They used chalk or white lead as make-up for their faces. The lead was poisonous and could make them ill.

Emerald and gold earrings

Children, slaves and working people all wore short tunics. Important men wore a heavy white robe called a **toga**. They wrapped it around their whole body and then over one shoulder.

Entertainment

The Romans loved watching **chariot** races at a place in Rome called the Circus Maximus. These were fast and very exciting. Sometimes the chariots crashed.

Roman charioteers

Romans also went to a big stadium called the Colosseum. Here they watched slaves and gladiators fight with each other until one was dead.

Every city had an open-air theatre. There were seats in a semi-circle around the stage. The actors wore masks. Most Romans liked funny plays, but there were sad plays too.

Going to the baths

Every Roman town had public baths for men and women. Romans went there every day to meet their friends and relax. They often started with some exercises or games. Then they went in the pools, the hot baths, the cold baths and steam rooms. They sometimes had a **massage**.

The Romans built bath houses at country villas and army forts. We can see Roman baths today at a city called Bath, in England.

The Roman baths in Bath

Cleaning up
Romans did not wash themselves with soap. They put oil on their bodies and then scraped their skin clean.

Roman children

Roman babies played with clay rattles in the shape of animals. Young children played with marbles and dolls.

At about seven years old, some boys and girls learned reading, writing and maths. They practised writing the alphabet. They used a sharp point to scrape the letters on boards covered in wax. If they made a mistake, they smoothed the wax and started again.

Lucky charms

When children were born, they were given a charm called a bulla. The charm protected them. Girls wore the charm until they married. Boys wore their charm until they were 16.

Some boys from rich families learned about history, poetry and making speeches. Some girls learned how to organize a home, how to sew and how to play a musical instrument with strings, called the cithara.

What happened to Rome?

The Romans fought their enemies for hundreds of years. It was difficult to rule such a large empire. Soldiers attacked the borders of the empire and some even attacked Rome. The city became less powerful and other people became kings.

Many of the things we do today started in ancient Rome. The languages we speak, our laws, our buildings, even our cooking would not be the same without Rome.

A worker uncovers the ruins of a Roman bath house.

ROMAN DATES

BC

753   Rome begins.

250   The Romans rule most of Italy.

58-50 Julius Caesar conquers Gaul (including modern-day France).

55-54 Julius Caesar attacks Britain.

44   Julius Caesar is murdered in Rome.

27   Emperors rule Rome.

AD

43   The Romans start to conquer Britain.

79   The volcano Vesuvius erupts in Italy.

117   The Roman empire is bigger than ever before.

330   Constantinople becomes capital of the Roman empire in the east.

410   Goths attack and capture Rome.

476   The Roman empire in the west comes to an end.

Glossary

banquet a big feast with invited guests

brooch a piece of jewellery with a pin, used to decorate or fasten clothing

chariot a light, fast carriage pulled by horses

conquer to beat an enemy

empire lots of lands ruled by a single ruler or nation

erupt to explode like a volcano

forum the business centre and meeting place in an ancient Roman town

general a senior army officer

legion a large battle unit in the Roman army

massage rubbing muscles to help relax the body

mosaic a picture with small pieces of coloured pottery, stone or glass

myth an old story about gods, goddesses, heroes or monsters

offering something given to honour or please a god

port a town by the sea, or on a lake or river, where ships can anchor

slave someone who is not free, and has to work for no money

spirit a magical being bringing good or bad luck

stola a long pleated dress worn over a tunic

thunderbolt a lightning flash and a roll of thunder

toga a white robe important men in Rome wore

villa a large Roman house

Index

army 8, 12

baths 24–25, 28

Caesar, Julius 13, 29

chariot 22

children 21, 26–27

clothes 12, 20–21

coins 10–11

Colosseum 22

empire, Roman 8–9, 28–29

food 18–19

France 4–5, 15

gods 14–15, 16

houses 16–17

mosaic 17

pirates 11

Pompeii 6–7

roads 9

Rome 8, 17, 22, 28–29

Romulus 9

ships 10–11

slaves 11, 18, 21, 22

soldiers 12–13

temple 15

theatre 23

toga 21

weapons 12